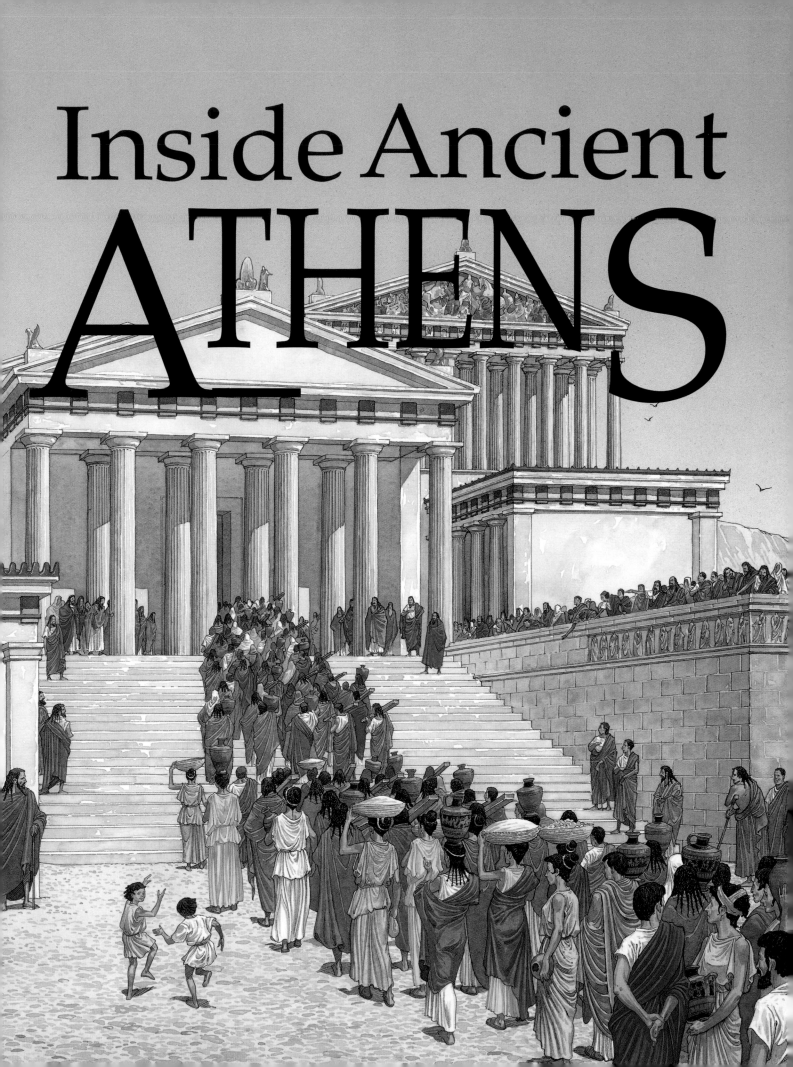

Inside Ancient
ATHENS

First American edition published in 2005 by
Enchanted Lion Books
45 Main Street, Suite 519
Brooklyn, NY 11201

© The Salariya Book Company Ltd MMV

ISBN 1-59270-044-6

Catalog-in-Publishing Data is on file with the Library of Congress

Author:
Fiona Macdonald studied history at Cambridge University and at the
University of East Anglia. She has taught in schools, adult education and
universities and is the author of numerous books for children on historical topics.

Artists:
David Antram was born in Brighton, England, in 1958. He studied at
Eastbourne College of Art and has illustrated many children's non-fiction books.

Mark Bergin was born in Hastings, England, in 1961. He studied at
Eastbourne College of Art and has specialised in historical reconstructions,
aviation and maritime subjects since 1983.

John James was born in London in 1959. He studied at Eastbourne College of
Art and has specialised in historical reconstruction since leaving art school in 1982.

Series Creator:
David Salariya was born in Dundee, Scotland. He has illustrated a wide range
of books and has created and designed many new series for publishers both in the
UK and overseas. In 1989, he established The Salariya Book Company. He lives
in Brighton with his wife, illustrator Shirley Willis, and their son Jonathan.

Editors: Penny Clarke, Claire Andrews

Printed and bound in China. Printed on paper from sustainable forests.
Manufactured by Leo Paper Products Ltd.

Photographic credits
b = bottom, c = centre, t = top

Ancient Art & Architecture Collection Ltd: 27c
The Art Archive: 24
The Art Archive / Acropolis Museum Athens / Dagli Orti: 23
The Art Archive / Agora Museum Athens / Dagli Orti: 25, 27t
The Art Archive / Archaeological Museum Piraeus / Dagli Orti: 33t
The Art Archive / British Museum / Eileen Tweedy: 33c
The Art Achive / Jan Vinchon Numismatist Paris / Dagli Orti: 6

The Art Archive / Kanellopoulos Museum Athens / Dagli Orti: 12
The Art Archive / Musée du Louvre Paris / Dagli Orti: 21, 40
The Art Archive / Museo di Villa Giulia Rome / Dagli Orti: 10
The Art Archive / Muzeo Nazionale Taranto / Dagli Orti: 35
The Art Archive / National Archaeological Museum Athens / Dagli Orti: 29
The Art Archive / National Museum Belgrade / Dagli Orti (A): 38

Every effort has been made to trace copyright holders. The Salariya Book
Company apologizes for any unintentional omissions and would be pleased,
in such cases, to add an acknowledgment in future editions.

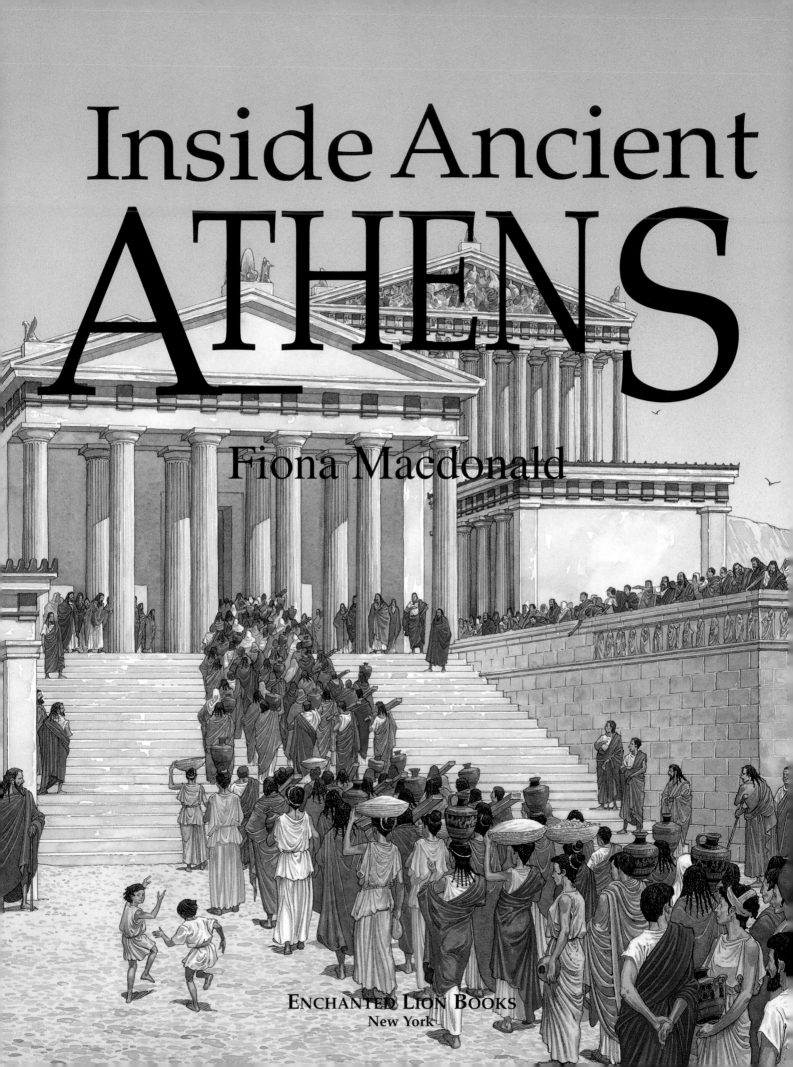

Inside Ancient
ATHENS

Fiona Macdonald

ENCHANTED LION BOOKS
New York

CONTENTS

Mainland Greece is a rugged peninsula of snow-capped mountains, steep valleys and little flat, fertile land. Around the coast are hundreds of rocky islands. In ancient times thick forests covered the hills. The surrounding seas are rough and stormy—the ancient Greeks rarely went to sea in the winter; earthquakes were and remain common. From around 775 BCE many families began to leave Greece in search of new homes and better farmland.

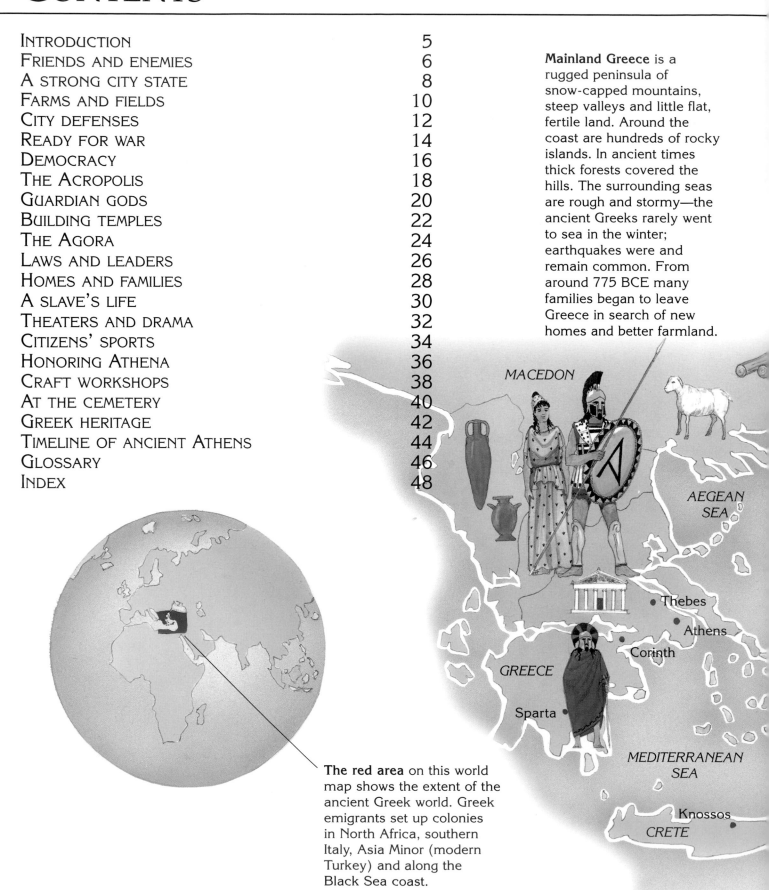

The red area on this world map shows the extent of the ancient Greek world. Greek emigrants set up colonies in North Africa, southern Italy, Asia Minor (modern Turkey) and along the Black Sea coast.

INTRODUCTION

The ancient Greeks were proud people: proud of their harsh country, their warriors, their iron and bronze weapons and wooden warships. They admired the work of their sculptors, puzzled over the new ideas their scientists and philosophers discussed and enjoyed the latest plays, poems and songs. They cheered at athletic competitions and when statues of their gods and goddesses were carried through the streets at festival time. But they were most proud of their language and system of government. They thought all non-Greeks were barbarians.

Greek civilization began around 2100 BCE when the Myceneans, a Greek-speaking people, arrived from the north and east and set up kingdoms. By around 800 BCE, after centuries of warfare, Greece was divided into many city-states. Then, from around 490 BCE until about 336 BCE, Athens dominated the rest and was the center of a brilliant civilization. New laws introduced the first democratic form of government. New buildings and statues in white marble made the city look spectacular. Discoveries by scientists and philosophers are still admired and respected today.

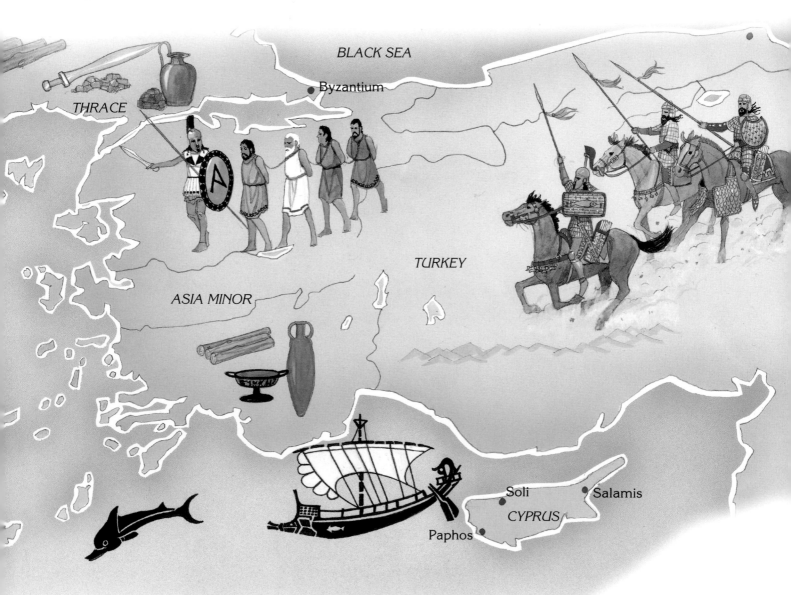

FRIENDS AND ENEMIES

Many different peoples lived in the Mediterranean region. They spoke different languages and followed different religions. Some, like the Egyptians, lived in vast empires. Others, like the Greeks, lived in small kingdoms or city-states. Sometimes all these peoples lived peacefully, trading with each other, exchanging new ideas, and copying new technologies. More often, however, they fought each other.

The most famous war was that between the Greeks and the Trojans from the city of Troy in Asia Minor (now Turkey), around 1250 BCE. But the Greeks' greatest enemies were the Persians (from the land now called Iran). In 499 BCE they invaded, hoping to make Greece part of their empire. The Greeks defeated them in 490 BCE, and again in 479 BCE after a second Persian invasion.

Silver coin with the head of the god Dionysos (above), made near Athens around 460 BCE. It was taken by traders to the Greek colony of Naxos, on the island of Sicily (off Italy's southern coast), where it was found by archaeologists.

The Trojan Horse (right) Greek poets, and in particular Homer, who lived around 750 BCE, told the story of the Trojan War as an exciting adventure. But historians now think that the Greeks and Trojans probably fought over trade. According to Homer the Greeks won the Trojan War by trickery. They built a huge hollow wooden horse. Many soldiers hid inside, while the rest (with one exception) sailed away. The soldier who stayed persuaded the Trojans to offer the horse to their gods. They dragged it inside the city. That night the Greek soldiers leapt out, attacked the Trojans and took the city.

Greek trading ships had sails to help them speed through open water, and oars to give the sailors greater control in harbors and shallow, dangerous seas close to shore.

A STRONG CITY-STATE

Between 499 BCE and 490 BCE Persian armies very nearly conquered Greece. But they failed, thanks to the bravery of Athenian *hoplites* (foot-soldiers), who defeated them at the Battle of Marathon in 490 BCE. The surviving Persians fled, but promised to return. How could Athens hope to defend itself for a second time?

In 483 BCE the city had an amazing stroke of luck. Miners discovered rich deposits of silver at Laurium, close to the city. The Athenian general Themistocles persuaded his fellow citizens to use this treasure to build a new navy with 200 magnificent warships.

Just as he had hoped, when the second Persian invasion came, these warships helped the Athenian navy defeat their enemy at the Battle of Salamis in 480 BCE. The silver also gave the Athenians power over other city-states in Greece—and money to rebuild their city in splendid style. This rebuilding was badly needed because the Persian attacks on Athens had caused terrible damage to the city. Work began in 479 BCE with the rebuilding of the city walls, houses and workshops, so people had homes and could earn their living. Then long walls were built to protect the road linking Athens with its port, Piraeus. After this, the citizens' democratic Assembly made plans for new public buildings around the *agora* (marketplace). Finally, in 447 BCE, work began on rebuilding the temples on the Acropolis.

FARMS AND FIELDS

Each city-state in Greece included areas of the countryside around it. Attica, the countryside around Athens, was typical of southern Greece: hilly, stony and dry. Very hot in summer, it could be bitterly cold in winter. Athenian farmers had to work hard to survive. Their chief crops were barley, olives, grapes and lentils. They kept sheep, goats, bees (for honey) and oxen (to pull carts and ploughs). In season, they gathered wild herbs, nuts, berries and mushrooms. But if they ventured too far into wild country, they risked attack from wolves, bears and wild boar.

City-states like Athens also had ports and harbors, used by merchants, fishermen and travellers. There were no wide roads, only narrow pathways. The quickest way to travel was often by sea, along the coast.

In autumn, ripe grapes were harvested and squashed by trampling underfoot. The juice that ran out was stored in wooden barrels. The natural yeasts and sugars fermented the juice, turning it into wine.

A well-built farmhouse in the countryside outside Athens (right). The walls were made of rough stones covered with plaster, and the roof of baked clay tiles. The rooms were arranged around a shady courtyard, secured with strong wooden gates. Greek farmers planted olive, fig and pear trees. Ripe olives were harvested by beating the trees to make the olives fall. Then they were gathered up and crushed between stones to extract the oil. This was used for cooking, eating, skin care and in medicines.

A man with a wine goblet (left) painted on an amphora about 520 BCE. His wreath of vine leaves shows he is intent on enjoying himself.

CITY DEFENSES

The city of Athens stood on a wide sprawling plain, about three miles from the coast. People first settled there around 5000 BCE, long before Greek-speakers arrived. By around 1250 BCE there was a fortress and a palace surrounded by rough walls of massive boulders. Remains of these were still visible in 500 BCE. The Athenians jokingly said they had been built by the Cyclops (one-eyed giants).

By 480 BCE, when the Persians invaded for a second time, the city of Athens had grown and spread over the plain below the Acropolis. It covered an area of just over one square mile. For the time, this was a very large area to defend. The new city walls, quickly built after the Persian invasion, were over four miles long.

The bronze arrowhead (far left) and spear-tip (left) were used by Athenian foot-soldiers around 550 BCE. They have long, sharp points and were originally fitted to wooden shafts. Both were designed to sink into enemy flesh, slicing muscles and cutting through veins. If the man they hit was not killed straight away, he often died later from infection or loss of blood.

Greek foot-soldiers (above left) were known as "hoplites," from "hoplon," the Greek word for a painted wooden shield. Hoplites also wore bronze helmets, leather or bronze greaves (leg-guards) and breastplates of bronze, padded linen or leather. Persian soldiers (above right) fought with bows and arrows, swords and spears. They carried large, light shields made of woven twigs covered with ox-hide.

Building the new city walls was a massive task. Greek writers tell how the Athenian general Themistocles ordered people to demolish old buildings and monuments—even tombs—so they had enough wood and building stone. The new walls had towers, look-out posts and 13 gates, where soldiers patrolled and watchmen kept guard. The main gate was in the north-west of the city, close to the district where craftworkers lived.

On the south-west of the city the new walls joined up with another great building project: the twin barriers called the Long Walls (completed in 458 BCE). These ran each side of the road between Athens and its port, Piraeus. They were designed to stop enemies cutting the city's link with food supplies brought in by sea.

READY FOR WAR

For much of the time between 461 and 338 BCE Athens was at war. From 461 to 404 BCE Athens fought the rival city-state of Sparta and its allies like Corinth. All Athenian men from the age of 18 to 60 had to be ready for war. Nobles fought on horseback. Ordinary citizens became hoplites. Men who could not afford armor fought as *psiloi* (bare) soldiers.

The Athenians' greatest victories were at sea: Salamis (480 BCE) against the Persians and Phormion (429 BCE) against the Corinthians. Pitched land battles, like the Battle of Marathon in 490 BCE, were rare. Fighting was usually a series of violent skirmishes between groups of soldiers.

Other tactics included destroying enemy crops, farms and livestock, and besieging their cities. In a siege, troops surrounded a city to cut off its food supply, so the people within starved.

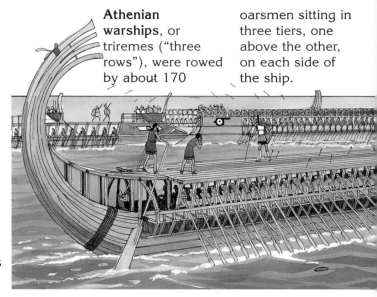

Athenian warships, or triremes ("three rows"), were rowed by about 170 oarsmen sitting in three tiers, one above the other, on each side of the ship.

Athenian soldiers had to provide their own weapons. If they could not afford weapons and armor they fought with sling-shots or bows and arrows. In battle, hoplites advanced in phalanx formation: in tight rows, shoulder to shoulder, with over-lapping shields and javelins pointing at the enemy. So long as they stood firm they were difficult to defeat. But if they panicked and ran, enemies could attack them one by one.

Athenians fought sea-battles in two different ways. They sailed alongside enemy ships so the soldiers waiting on deck could jump across and fight. Or they rowed fast at an enemy ship to smash a hole in its hull with the trireme's battering ram.

The biggest triremes were about 49 yards long and 20 feet wide. At full speed they could travel at 10 miles an hour.

Triremes were made of wood, with linen sails. They were steered with huge oars at the stern (back). At the prow (front) each one had a sharp battering ram to hole enemy ships just below the water line, so they would sink.

DEMOCRACY

I n 508 BCE Athens became a democracy—
a state governed by its citizens. Each
citizen shared in the city's government by
attending the Assembly, being members
of the Council, or one of the ten Generals who
led the army and upheld the laws. But only
free-born adult males from Athenian families
could be citizens; foreigners, women and
slaves could not, even though they made up
the majority of the population. Democracy,
introduced by the Athenian leader Kleisthenes,
helped end the feuds between rival nobles.

The Council (Boule) had
500 members, all over 30
years old. They suggested
policies to debate in the
Assembly and carried out
decisions made there.
They were responsible for
city buildings, and for
supplying the army
and navy.

Council meetings were
held in the Council
House (*bouleuterion*)
and were open to the
public. Groups of 50
councillors took turns
being on duty day and
night, to deal with
any emergency.

The Assembly met every ten days to discuss important issues, such as whether to go to war. It also made laws. About 5,000 citizens attended each meeting, and voting was by a show of hands. Each citizen could speak at Assembly meetings, but they were not all good at making speeches. So citizens who wanted to persuade the others to agree with their views either studied public speaking or hired expert speakers (*rhetors*) to make speeches for them. The speakers stood on a rostrum (raised stone platform) so they could be seen and heard. Athenians were proud of their democracy, and Council meetings were always well attended.

At first the Assembly met in the *agora* (the marketplace). But from about 500 BCE members gathered on a hill called the Pnyx (Crowded Place). Meetings lasted less than a day and were abandoned if it rained.

Citizens could remove a politician they disapproved of by "ostracizing" him. They wrote his name on an *ostrakon* (a piece of broken pottery often used for making rough notes), and dropped it into a large pottery jar. If more than 6,000 pieces with the politician's name on were collected, he was banished from Athens for ten years. The name "Themistocles" is on this ostrakon (right).

THE ACROPOLIS

The Acropolis is a rugged hill, about 50 feet high, that towers above Athens. For thousands of years its impressive size made it a holy place. By 600 BCE Athenians were worshipping the goddess Athena there.

The cliffs of the Acropolis also made it a safe stronghold. Around 1250 BCE a fortress was built at the top, with a palace nearby. In 490 BCE the Athenians built a temple to Athena on the Acropolis, to give thanks for their victory over the Persians. Called the Parthenon (Temple of the Maiden), it housed an ancient wooden statue of Athena. But this temple was destroyed when the Persians attacked again in 479 BCE. Then, in 447 BCE, Athenians voted to build a new temple, and to add many other new buildings to the Acropolis.

The Parthenon (10) was built in just ten years. It housed a majestic statue of Athena, made of gold and ivory. A second giant statue of Athena (6) stood outside. It could be seen by sailors far out at sea.

1. *Propylaea* (great gateway)
2. Temple of Nike (goddess of victory)
3. *Eleusinion* (temple of Demeter, goddess of fertility)
4. *Brauronia* (sanctuary of Artemis, goddess of childbirth and virginity)
5. *Chalcothece* (treasury; store for holy objects used in temples)
6. Giant bronze statue of Athena (29 1/2 feet high)
7. *Pandroseion* (temple of the goddess of mysteries)
8. Erectheion (temple of Poseidon and Athena)
9. Altar of Athena
10. Parthenon (temple of Athena)
11. Sanctuary of Zeus (king of the gods)

THE ACROPOLIS 19

Guardian Gods

Artemis, fierce virgin goddess of hunting, the moon and childbirth.

Apollo, god of music, poetry, drama, the sun and the sky.

Ares, hot-tempered god of war, rage, battles and bloodshed.

Dionysos, god of wine, pleasure, madness and creativity.

Aphrodite, charming, thoughtless goddess of love and beauty.

Athena, goddess of wisdom who protected the city of Athens.

Like other Greeks, the Athenians honored local gods and goddesses, who they believed lived in rocky places, streams and trees. They also honored past heroes and heroines. Some may have been real people, who ruled Greek kingdoms long ago, or warriors who had died bravely in battle. The Greeks also believed 12 powerful gods and goddess lived on Mount Olympus in northern Greece. They protected all the Greeks, but favored certain city-states. Athenians believed they were guarded and guided by Athena.

According to ancient myths Athena was the daughter of Zeus, king of the gods. Unmarried, she was clever, stern and wise. She protected all craftworkers, and had brought the olive tree to Attica. (Without olives, Athens would have had difficulty surviving.) Her great rival was Poseidon, god of the sea, who was worshipped in the countryside.

The Greeks believed temples were the homes of gods and goddesses. To please them, they left gifts of fine craftwork, food and wine at the temples. Greek priests also sacrificed animals at altars outside temples. They burnt the skin and bones on the altar, saying the smoke carried them up to the gods. The meat was cooked separately and shared among worshippers.

Zeus, mighty god of thunder and lightning and king of the gods.

Hera, jealous wife of Zeus. Goddess of women and female animals.

Hephaestus, strong, clever god of black-smiths, weapons and tools.

Hestia, guardian goddess of family fires, hearths and homes.

Hermes, bright, quick and a trickster. Messenger of the gods.

Poseidon, terrifying god of storms, earthquakes and the sea.

A priest holding a large knife (right), and his helper, ready to sacrifice a pig on an altar outside a temple.

BUILDING TEMPLES

The first temples were made of wood, just like early Greek houses. They were constructed from tree-trunks, with wooden poles or planks for the roof. Later temples were built of stone, though the design stayed the same, with stone columns replacing the tree-trunks. Stone was stronger, lasted longer and the Greeks thought it was more beautiful. It could be cut into patterns and carved into wonderful pictures.

But stone was hard to work with. Greek stonemasons had no powerful machines to clear land for building, or to cut stone from quarries and transport it to building sites. Instead, they relied on muscle-power.

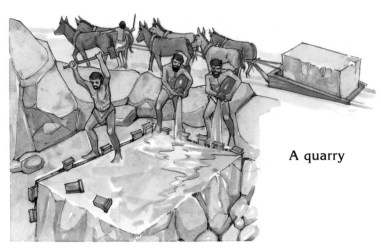

A quarry

Stone for Athens' new temples came from quarries at Mount Pentelicus in the countryside nearby.

It took 22,000 tons of marble (fine smooth stone) to build the Parthenon. This was paid for by tribute (tax) collected from weaker Greek cities.

Mules and oxen pulled carts; workers and slaves hauled on ropes to drag sledges. It took ten years for teams of laborers to build the new Parthenon temple on the Acropolis in Athens. That was very quick by the standards of the time, but that was because it was such an important temple.

Blocks of stone and sections of pillars were cut roughly to shape at the quarry, then dragged up sloping ramps to the waiting carts. Once at the building site they were trimmed to their final shape.

After trimming, the sections of the columns were fitted together. They were held in place with wooden pegs in the center. Roofs were made of wooden beams covered with clay tiles or thin slabs of marble.

Below the roof of the Parthenon and running around all four sides was a decorated frieze - a wide band of stonework made up of brightly painted marble sculptures. The friezes depicted scenes from Greek legends. The relief below comes from the east side and shows the gods Poseidon, Apollo and Artemis.

Columns in Greek temples look straight.

But in fact they are curved and lean inwards.

If they weren't, the temple would appear to bend.

The Agora

The agora, a big open space in the center of Athens, was the city's heart. Every day it was thronged with people (mostly men), talking about business, discussing the latest ideas or just watching the street entertainers.

Housewives shopped at the food stalls or looked at expensive goods, like cloth and shoes, in shops in *stoas* (covered porches and arcades) on three sides of the agora.

Around the agora were government buildings, including the mint, a debtors' prison, the law courts, temples to Apollo, Aphrodite and Hephaestus, the Council House and the *tholos* (lodgings for Council members on 24-hour duty). There was an altar to the 12 most important gods and a public fountain.

Athenian merchants rarely accepted coins from other city-states. They preferred the pure silver coins of Athens. This coin (above) shows the head of the goddess Persephone.

Most of the buildings around the agora were built about 460 BCE, although a few were added after the Parthenon temple was finished in 432 BCE. Then trees were planted in the agora to give shade in the hot Athenian summers.

Like many other fine public works in Athens, these were built by and for the citizens. The money for them came from the tribute paid by weaker cities in return for Athenian leadership and protection in times of war.

These lead weights, (right) once used by ancient Athenian traders, were found in the agora. They would have been used to weigh out goods for sale. The Council employed officials to check that traders used accurate weights. Anyone caught cheating was banned. Ancient Greeks measured dry materials in "talents" (about 67 pounds).

Women from rich families did not visit the agora. It was shameful for them to appear in public, except at religious festivals.

But female traders, entertainers, slaves and ordinary housewives all joined the busy crowds there.

LAWS AND LEADERS

Besides making laws, Athenian citizens judged criminals. All citizens could serve on juries to decide if a person was guilty or not. The juries were large; depending on the case, they could have between 201 and 2500 members. To become a juror, men met in the agora on the day fixed for a trial (around 200 were held every year). Each had a bronze ticket bearing his name, his father's name and the name of his clan. Officials pushed these into a machine called a *kleroterion* to select or reject them.

Important trials took place in the *heliaia* (court building) on the south-west side of the Agora. There were no state prosecutors or lawyers; anyone could—and did—accuse another man or woman of a crime. Accused people had the right to defend themselves and many hired respected thinkers to write their speeches, or invited witnesses to give evidence in their favor.

Leaders of the Athenian community—Council members or Army generals—often made powerful speeches in the law courts and the Assembly. It was a way of impressing the citizens, and increasing their influence in the city's government.

Water clock

This *clepsydra* (pottery water-clock) (right) was used to time speeches in Athenian courts. At the beginning of each speech it was filled to the brim. When all the water had run out of the little holes at the bottom – which took about six minutes – the speaker had to stop.

Ballots

At a trial each juror was given two ballots (metal disks). The one with the hollow center meant "guilty," the other one "not guilty." At the end of the case jurors gave their verdict by dropping one of their ballots into a pottery jar.

A *kleroterion* (above) was a machine for selecting jurors. Court officials pushed the bronze ticket belonging to each citizen into a slot in the machine. Then they dropped black or white marbles into the machine down metal tubes. If a white marble landed against a row of tickets, the men named on them were chosen for jury service that day. If a black marble landed against their names, they were told to go away and come back another time.

HOMES AND FAMILIES

Most Greek households were large —even though the average house in a city-state like Athens was usually rather small. Three generations usually lived together— grandparents, parents and children—as well as live-in servants or slaves. All Greek families, except the very poorest, owned several slaves.

The head of the household was always a man, who had great power over other family members. Husbands and wives relied on each other to earn a living (men's work), run a household and rear children (women's work), and worship the household gods (together). Marriage for most Greeks was a practical arrangement rather than a matter of love or personal choice. Men were valued for their money, war-record or political connections. Girls were chosen for their dowries (money paid by their father when they married) or (everyone hoped) as mothers of sons.

Greek food was simple, but very healthy. People ate lots of brown bread, served with small helpings of fresh fish, seafood or cheese. They also enjoyed olives, nuts, beans, garlic and herbs.

For dessert, there were fresh or dried figs, grapes, apples, pears or sticky honey-cakes. The Greeks drank wine with their meals, but they usually mixed it with plenty of water.

A large house like this, with several rooms, would probably have belonged to a successful craftsman.

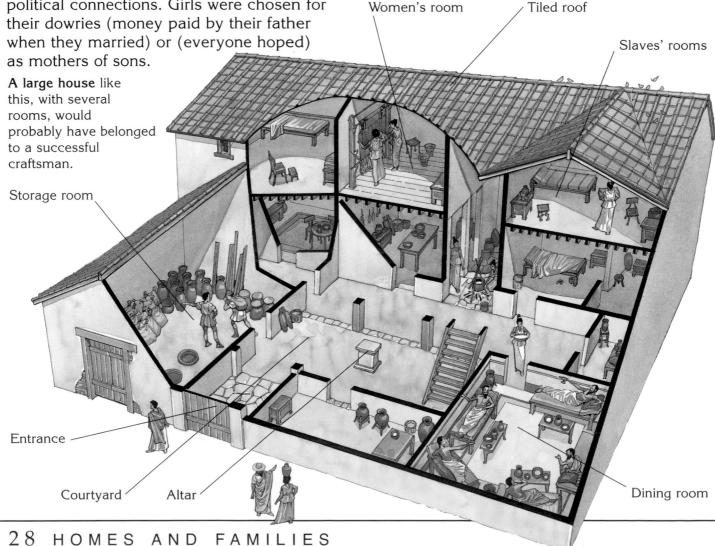

Women's room

Tiled roof

Slaves' rooms

Storage room

Entrance

Courtyard

Altar

Dining room

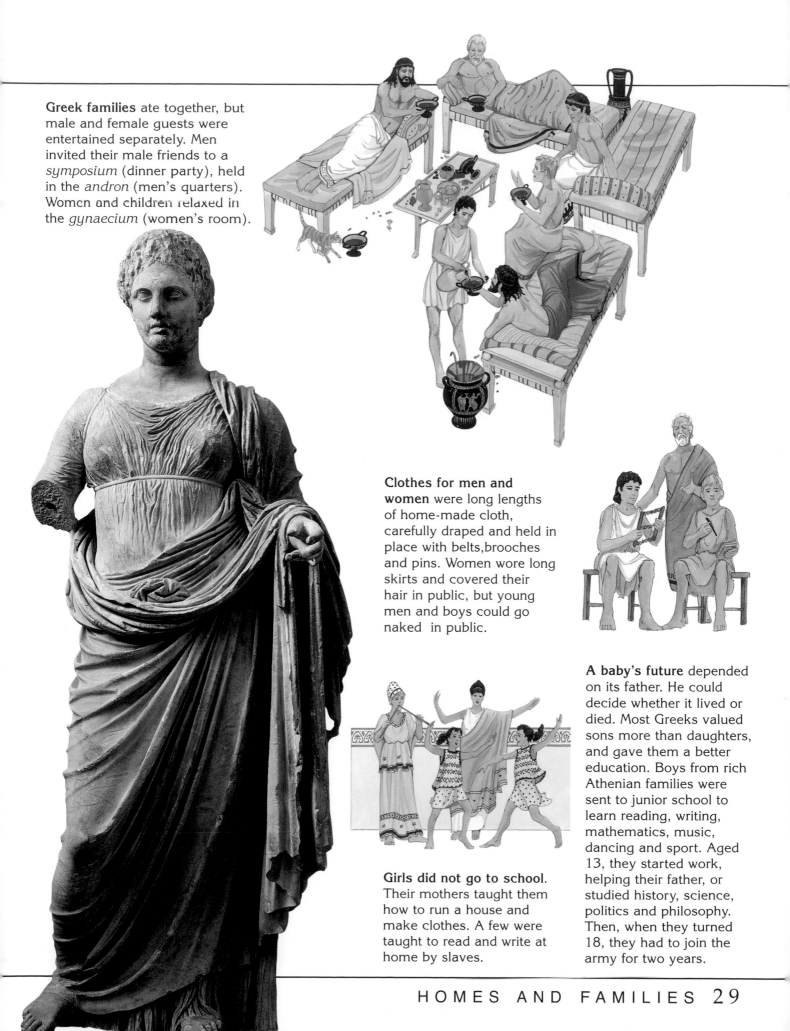

Greek families ate together, but male and female guests were entertained separately. Men invited their male friends to a *symposium* (dinner party), held in the *andron* (men's quarters). Women and children relaxed in the *gynaecium* (women's room).

Clothes for men and women were long lengths of home-made cloth, carefully draped and held in place with belts, brooches and pins. Women wore long skirts and covered their hair in public, but young men and boys could go naked in public.

Girls did not go to school. Their mothers taught them how to run a house and make clothes. A few were taught to read and write at home by slaves.

A baby's future depended on its father. He could decide whether it lived or died. Most Greeks valued sons more than daughters, and gave them a better education. Boys from rich Athenian families were sent to junior school to learn reading, writing, mathematics, music, dancing and sport. Aged 13, they started work, helping their father, or studied history, science, politics and philosophy. Then, when they turned 18, they had to join the army for two years.

A SLAVE'S LIFE

In Athens and many other city-states, at least a quarter of the population were slaves. Men, women and children became slaves in different ways. Most non-Greek slaves were from Asia Minor, North Africa or lands around the Black Sea and had been captured by enemies or raiding slave-traders. Some slaves were the children of slaves working for Greek families. Others were free-born Greeks condemned to slavery as punishment for serious crimes. Free Greeks with large debts sometimes sold themselves to the people to whom they owed money. They hoped to buy back their freedom later.

Greek society depended on slaves. They worked on farms, in workshops and homes. In Athens, male slaves worked on building projects, such as making roads, and as expert craftsmen. Forty thousand male slaves dug for silver in the mines at Laurium. Their lives were terrible and usually short. The heat in the mines was unbearable and the air was full of poisonous fumes.

Most women slaves did the usual female tasks: cooking, cleaning, making clothes and caring for children. But some were forced to work as prostitutes. They faced abuse, humiliation and disease.

You are born to a non-Greek family. Your mother and father are free people.

As a child you are taken captive by enemies and carried away for ever.

Your captors sell you to Greek slave-traders who are visiting their city.

They drag you on board a ship. The weather is stormy and you are very seasick.

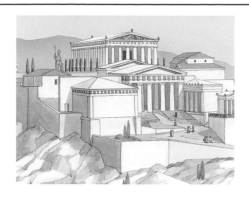

You're relieved to reach land, but shocked to be put in chains. The size of the buildings around the Agora amazes you.

You are put on sale alongside criminals, captives, debtors and the children of slaves.

Some men are bought by farmers, others by builders or road-makers. Some are bought as household slaves.

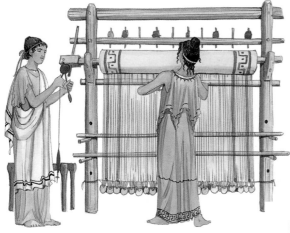

Slave women are sold as cooks, cleaners, nurse-maids, ladies' maids and entertainers. Pretty girls were always the first to be bought in the slave-market.

You are bought by a craftsman potter. Your first task is to sweep his studio. You work alongside many other slaves. Some have been trained to throw pots or fire kilns.

Your master treats you well. He gives you food, bedding and sometimes a small coin. But if you do something silly or wrong, he beats you severely or denies you food.

After many years you get promoted. Your master now trusts you to sell his pottery.

But you have no rights and cannot own property because **you** are property.

You're old, and can't work any longer. You feel sick, tired and miserable. When you're dead and buried in an unmarked grave, who will remember you?

THEATERS AND DRAMA

The first Greek dramas (plays) were performed at temples in honor of the gods. In Athens they were part of festivals for Dionysos, god of pleasure and wine. They retold ancient myths, stories about famous heroes and exciting events in history. The actors were all men and a chorus (a group of singers and dancers) commented on the action.

These early dramas were so popular that many Greek cities built large open-air theaters where plays were performed to large audiences. Performances lasted all day and often ended with rude dances by actors dressed as satyrs (mythical monsters—half-man and half-horse or goat).

Very few women went to the theater because the Greeks thought some plays were too rude, and others too frightening, for women to see. Slaves were also banned from going. Going to the theater was very cheap, and sometimes even free, because city governments or rich citizens paid for the performances.

Three of the world's greatest dramatists lived in Athens between 500 and 400 BCE. Aristophanes wrote comedies that made fun of the city's leaders and other citizens and their wives. Sophocles and Euripides both wrote powerful tragedies. Today, over two thousand years later, their plays are still performed all over the world.

Greek theater masks. Actors wore comic (bottom) or tragic (top) masks depending on the part they were playing.

The Theater of Dionysos in Athens could seat 14,000 spectators. Like other theaters, it was designed in a half-circle, with seats hollowed out like steps into a steep hillside. This helped actors' voices carry right to the back rows. Actors wore masks, wigs and colorful costumes, and stood on a raised platform (the *proscenium*). The chorus danced in an open space (the *orchestra*) in front of them.

CITIZENS' SPORTS

The Greeks thought sports were important – to please the gods, to keep fit and to train for war. The most famous games, first held at Olympia in 776 BCE, honored Zeus, king of the gods. In Athens, sports were part of a festival for the goddess Athena. Sport was taught at most boys' schools, together with energetic dancing. Large cities like Athens had public gymnasiums, where teenage boys and men trained. Young men joining the army also played sports, to make sure they were tough enough.

Popular Greek sports were running, wrestling, throwing the discus and javelin, boxing, long-jumping, and chariot-racing. The most dangerous was "pankration" (total power), a violent combination of boxing and wrestling. No holds were barred and only biting and gouging out the eyes were banned. Winners received wreaths of olive-leaves, ribbons and valuable gifts such as fine cloth and olive oil. Coming first was all that mattered. Only the winner received prizes. Top athletes became famous, and brought honor to their city-states and families.

Competitors in the *hoplitodromos* wore helmets and carried heavy shields. Like other Greek athletes, they trained and raced with no clothes on. Greek clothes were too loose and trailing and would have gotten in the way.

In the long jump athletes ran to the starting line, then sprang forward from a standing start. In each hand they held a heavy stone weight which they swung to help them jump further.

Hurling the javelin also began as training for war. Competitors threw wooden spears, about 6 1/2 feet long, as far as they could.

A discus (circular metal plate) weighed about 6 1/2 pounds, and measured about 10 inches in diameter. The best athletes could throw one almost 98 feet.

As part of their training, athletes used to lift heavy weights to build their muscles and make them stronger.

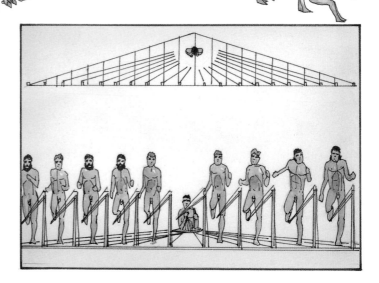

Runners took up position behind a starting gate formed of two cords stretched across the track. The starter would shout "Apite!" (Go!) and release a cord, which catapulted the gate to the ground.

Wrestlers shown on an Athenian amphora (opposite). This special jar, full of olive oil, was given to winners at the Panathenaic Games.

HONORING ATHENA

Every year the people of Athens watched as the old moon waned in the month of Hetakombion (June/July). The new moon signalled the start of the city's greatest religious festival, the Panathenaia. Athenians celebrated over 40 festivals each year. Some honored gods and goddesses or spirits hidden underground. Some were ancient rituals, surviving from the time when Athens was ruled by kings. Some, like Skira (harvest), praised nature. Others, such as Anthesteria (children's festival), marked important stages in people's lives. All the festivals made Athenians feel proud of their city, and closer to the gods. But the Panathenaia was the most important, because it honored Athena, the city's own goddess.

The high point of the Panathenaia was the procession through the city to the Parthenon, Athena's temple on the Acropolis. Girls carried presents for the goddess, while men and boys led animals to be sacrificed. After they had been sacrificed everyone feasted on the meat. Every four years there was an extra celebration, the Grand Panathenaia, when Athena's statue was given a new robe. The festival included competitions in music, drama, dancing and sport. These were a way of offering the city's best things to Athena, and asking her to bless them.

CRAFT WORKSHOPS

Although wealthy men in city-states like Athens despised people who worked for a living and made things with their hands, they admired the goods they produced, such as bronze weapons, gold jewellery and fine pottery.

Athenian pottery was prized at home and abroad. Between 500 and 400 BCE, Athenian potters made nearly all of the best pottery used in the Greek world. The part of Athens where potters worked was known as Kerameikos (potters' place), from which the word "ceramic" comes. Most craftworkers were men, employed in workshops owned by a master craftsman. Some were free and were paid; others were slaves. The largest-known workshop had about 120 free workers and 50 slaves. Women specialized in spinning and weaving to make clothes, blankets and rugs. Free-born or slave, they usually worked at home.

This gold bracelet, made about 550 BCE, has rope-like decorations and a pair of snakes' heads. Gold jewellery was made by casting the molten gold in moulds. Patterns were engraved (cut into) or stamped on it.

Athenian pots were thrown on wheels, then painted in the latest fashion. Around 900 BCE geometric patterns were popular, then, from 700 BCE, pictures of fruit and flowers. From 570 BCE animals and people painted in black on the red clay were popular. Then, after 500 BCE, the background was painted black, with the figures left unpainted and red. The best potters became famous, signing each pot with their name.

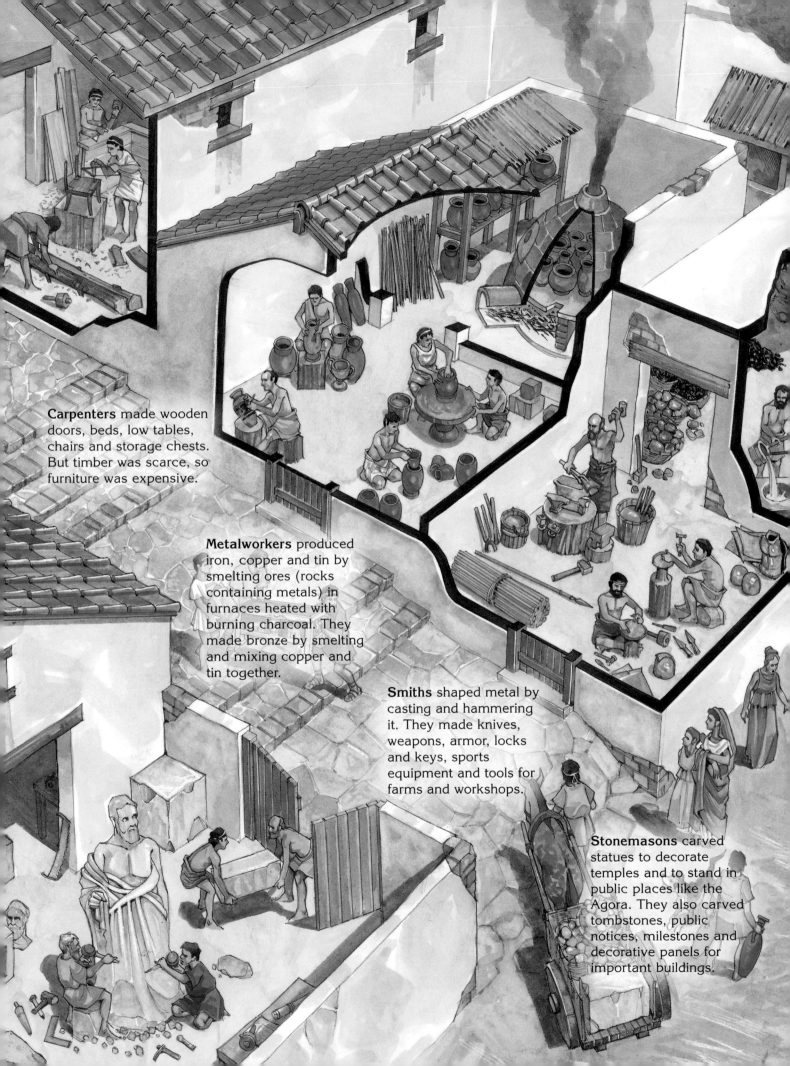

Carpenters made wooden doors, beds, low tables, chairs and storage chests. But timber was scarce, so furniture was expensive.

Metalworkers produced iron, copper and tin by smelting ores (rocks containing metals) in furnaces heated with burning charcoal. They made bronze by smelting and mixing copper and tin together.

Smiths shaped metal by casting and hammering it. They made knives, weapons, armor, locks and keys, sports equipment and tools for farms and workshops.

Stonemasons carved statues to decorate temples and to stand in public places like the Agora. They also carved tombstones, public notices, milestones and decorative panels for important buildings.

AT THE CEMETERY

In ancient Greece death was always close. Men died in battle, women died in childbirth, and children died from accidents or infections. Whole cities might face sudden mass death and suffering. This happened in war, and also in epidemics, as when plague (a killer disease) struck Athens from 430–429 BCE. Although some strong, healthy—and lucky—people survived until they were over 70, most died before they were 50.

The Greeks believed that each human body had a soul. But they did not all agree on what happened to a soul after the body died. Some said that souls lived in tombs and needed feeding with sacrifices brought by living members of their families. Others thought that souls went to the Underworld, a shadowy place ruled by the gloomy god Hades and guarded by a monstrous dog, Cerberus. Souls only survived in Hades while living people remembered them. If forgotten, they faded away. So statues, tombstones and carved lists of dead heroes—especially soldiers—were important to help souls stay alive.

The Greeks also believed it was very important to have correct funeral — ceremonies. Without them, a soul could not break free from its dead body and would haunt the place where it had died.

In Athens, after mourning and sacrifices, bodies were buried in cemeteries outside the city's walls.

A dead body was bathed, blessed with oil, dressed and draped with garlands of leaves and flowers. Three days later it was wrapped in a shroud, draped in a cloak and laid on a bier. It was taken to the cemetery in a solemn procession, then cremated (burnt to ash) or buried. Mourners made offerings of oil, wine and water to the dead person's soul, and ate a solemn meal with it, beside the grave.

Some Greeks said that a soul died at the same time as the body, or that it moved on to live in another living creature. But not many people believed these ideas.

GREEK HERITAGE

In 338 BCE the Greek city-states were invaded from Macedonia (a kingdom to the north). Then, in 146 BCE, the Romans conquered Greece, the city-states collapsed, and Greece became part of the Roman Empire. But Greek civilization did not die. The Romans and Macedonians admired Greek art, science and learning. They let the Greeks keep their culture and traditions, and employed the best Greek doctors, scholars, artists and engineers. In this way, Greek knowledge, ideas, styles and designs were preserved.

After the Roman Empire collapsed around 500 CE, Christian rulers and church leaders in Byzantium (now Istanbul, Turkey) continued to treasure Greek learning. So did Muslim scholars in Spain, North Africa and the Middle East. Around 1400 CE scholars from western Europe "rediscovered" ancient Greek and Roman civilization. They studied Greek and Roman writings, architecture and art. Because of this, the years from around 1400 to 1600 CE are known as the "Renaissance" (rebirth) of ancient culture.

Today, the ancient Greeks still influence us. All over the world people use their words, think about their ideas, rely on inventions and discoveries their scientists made and copy their designs.

Ancient Greek ideas about medicine have guided Europeans for centuries. Hippocrates (born 460 BCE), the most famous Greek doctor, is still known as "the Father of Medicine." He questioned earlier theories—for example, that illness was sent by the gods—and taught that good food, fresh air and exercise would help people stay healthy.

Hippocrates carefully observed his patients and their illnesses, and noted which medicines helped to cure them. Around 400 BCE he set up a school for doctors. His students took an oath (made a solemn promise) to use their skills to heal, not to harm. This oath, known as the Hippocratic oath, still underpins medical training.

Today, people still admire ancient Greek ideas, such as democracy. Many states and international organizations are based upon democratic principles. They copy Athenian traditions, such as public debate and voting to make important decisions. Their buildings, such as the United Nations General Assembly Hall in New York (right), have also been influenced by ancient Greek designs, including the Council house in Athens and Greek open-air theaters.

Ancient Greek buildings —especially the Parthenon in Athens— have been copied all around the world. This is the New York Stock Exchange in lower Manhattan. Its pillars and carvings were designed to remind viewers of ancient Greek ideas, as well as their artistic styles.

The Ancient Greek Games, held every four years at Olympia in honor of Zeus, inspired the modern Olympic Games. First held in 1896, they include both new sports and ancient Greek ones. Unlike the original Olympics, women can take part.

Many modern words are based on ancient Greek ones, for example:

Ceramic
Cylinder
Dinosaur

Geography
Mega
Music
Myth
Orchestra
Photography
Pylon
Skeleton
Telephone
Television
Theory

TIMELINE OF ANCIENT ATHENS

c. 6000 BCE First farmers settle on the Greek mainland.

c. 2000 BCE Mainland Greece is controlled by kings from the powerful Minoan culture based on the island of Crete.

c. 2100 BCE The first Greek-speaking people (later known as the Myceneans) arrive on mainland Greece.

c. 1600–1100 BCE Mycenean warrior kings rule many small kingdoms on mainland Greece. They fight the earlier inhabitants.

c. 1400 BCE Minoan palace-cities on Crete are destroyed, by an earthquake or volcanic eruption.

c. 1250 BCE Possible date of Trojan War, fought by Greeks against Troy in Asia Minor.

c. 1200 BCE End of Mycenean civilization.

c. 1200 BCE Knowledge of iron-working spreads among Greek-speakers. With better weapons, they take control of Greece.

c. 1100–900 BCE Wars among Greek rulers disrupt farming and cause hardship in Greece.

c. 800 BCE By now Greece is divided into many small city-states, each ruled by its own king or noble family. Greek civilization begins to recover.

c. 800–700 BCE A poet (today known as Homer) writes down earlier stories about wars, gods, heroes and monsters. These are called the *Iliad* and the *Odyssey*.

c. 776 BCE Traditionally the date of the first Olympic Games.

c. 750–500 BCE Greek families leave the Greek mainland to settle in colonies around the Mediterranean Sea.

650–500 BCE Tyrants (single powerful rulers) or oligarchies (groups of rich men) take control of the government of many city-states.

c. 508 BCE Athens starts to become a democracy. Every adult male citizen has the right to speak at Assemblies and to vote.

499–490 BCE First Persian invasion of Greece.

496–406 BCE Lifetime of Sophocles, Athens's most famous dramatist.

495–429 BCE Lifetime of Pericles, the general who led Athens at the height of its power.

483 BCE Silver found at Laurium near Athens.

482 BCE Athens starts to build a fleet of warships.

480–479 BCE Second Persian invasion. Athens attacked and badly damaged.

469–399 BCE Lifetime of Socrates, Athenian teacher and philosopher.

460–360 BCE Time of great achievements in art and learning, especially in Athens.

447–438 BCE Parthenon temple built in Athens. All the sculptures were in place by 432 BCE.

431–404 BCE Peloponnesian War between rival Greek city-states.

404 BCE Sparta defeats Athens and becomes the most powerful city-state on mainland Greece.

371 BCE Sparta is defeated by Thebes, which becomes the most powerful Greek city-state.

362 BCE Sparta and Athens join forces to defeat Thebes.

338 BCE Troops from Macedonia (a state north of Greece) invade and conquer mainland Greek city-states.

336–323 BCE Alexander the Great of Macedonia conquers an empire from Greece to India.

300–200 BCE Greek civilization continues in Greek colonies around the Mediterranean Sea, and spreads overland through Afghanistan to India.

287–211 BCE Lifetime of Archimedes, Greek mathematician, scientist and inventor.

279 BCE Greece invaded by armies of Celts from north-west Europe.

275 BCE Roman armies take control of many Greek colonies.

168 BCE Romans defeat the Macedonian rulers of mainland Greece.

146 BCE Romans conquer mainland Greece.

GLOSSARY

Acropolis the steep hill in Athens on which temples were built.

agora meeting place (also the marketplace) in the center of a Greek city.

andron room in a Greek house where men were entertained.

Assembly (Ekklesia) the main decision-making body in Athens. It met every day to discuss government plans. It also appointed officials to run the city.

barbarians the Greeks' name for foreigners. They said that non-Greek languages sounded like "bar-bar-bar."

bier a cart, or similar form of transport, on which a body is put and carried to the cemetery for burial or cremation.

bronze metal made by melting tin and copper together. The Greeks used it to make armor.

cavalry soldiers who fought on horseback.

chorus group of actors who comment on the main events in a Greek drama.

citizen person who lives in a city or state and has rights as a member of the community there. Only men could be citizens in ancient Greece.

city-state a city and the countryside around it, ruled as a separate state with its own laws and government. There were about 300 city-states in ancient Greece.

civilization a society with its own laws, customs, beliefs and artistic traditions.

colony settlement of people living outside their home country. The Greeks founded many colonies.

democracy system of government in which all citizens have the right to share in making government decisions.

greaves leg-armor.

gynaecium private room for women only.

hoplites Greek foot-soldiers.

juror member of the public who attends a trial in a law court to decide whether the accused person is guilty of the crime.

kleroterion machine used to select jurors at law courts in Athens.

Mount Olympus mountain in northern Greece. Home of the Greek gods and goddesses.

myths traditional stories about gods, heroes and monsters. They usually have a religious, moral or political meaning.

offerings goods given to gods and goddesses to ask for help or give thanks for blessings.

oligarchs rich male rulers.

olive fruit of the olive tree. Olives were eaten as food or crushed to make oil.

ostracism voting to banish an unpopular politician from Athens for ten years.

palace-city earlier, and smaller, form of the city-state, centered around a palace rather than a city. Knossos on the island of Crete was an important palace-city.

Panathenaia festival held in Athens to honor the goddess Athena.

pankration violent form of wrestling.

Parthenon temple of the goddess Athena on the Acropolis in Athens.

phalanx battle-formation of foot-soldiers, standing closely side by side.

philosophy the search for, and study of, knowledge, wisdom and truth.

sacrifice killing an animal as an offering to the gods.

satyrs rough, rude mythical monsters, half man and half horse or goat.

shroud length of cloth in which a dead body is wrapped before cremation or burial.

slaves men, women and children who are not free, but are owned by other people.

tholos lodgings near the Agora for Council members when they were on 24-hour duty.

trireme Greek warship rowed by three tiers of oarsmen.

tyrant powerful man who ruled alone and usually ignored earlier laws.

Underworld according to Greek belief, the place where the spirits of dead people went after death.

INDEX

A

Acropolis 9, 12, 18-19, 22, 37, 46
agora 9, 17, 24-5, 26, 31, 39, 46, 47
Alexander the Great 45
animals 10, 14, 20, 21, 37, 38
armor 12, 14, 39, 46
army 16, 26, 29, 34
art and architecture 5, 42, 45
Assembly 9, 16, 17, 26, 44, 46
Athena 18, 19, 20, 34, 36-7, 47
Attica 10, 20

B

barbarians 5
Byzantium 42

C

children 28, 29, 30, 31, 36, 40
citizens 8, 14, 16, 17, 25, 26, 27, 32, 33, 44, 46
city-states 5, 6, 8-9, 10, 14, 20, 28, 30, 34, 38, 42, 44, 45
city walls 9, 12-13, 40
clothing 24, 29, 38
coins 6, 24, 31
colonies 6, 44, 45, 46
Corinth, Corinthians 14
Council 16, 25, 26
Council House (bouleterion) 16, 24, 42
craftworkers 13, 20, 28, 30, 31, 38-9

D, E

democracy 5, 9, 16-17, 42, 44, 46

education 29

F

families 25, 28-9, 30, 40
farming 10-11, 14, 30, 31, 39, 44
festivals 5, 25, 32, 34, 36-7, 47
food and drink 10, 13, 20, 24, 28, 31, 40, 47
funerals 40-1

G

gods and goddesses 5, 6, 18, 19, 20-1, 24, 28, 32, 33, 34, 36, 37, 40, 46, 47
government 5, 16, 26, 32, 44, 46

H, J, K

homes, houses 9, 10, 11, 22, 28-9, 30

juries, jurors 26, 27, 46

kings 19, 36, 44
Kleisthenes 16

L

Laurium 8, 30, 45
laws 5, 16, 17, 26-7, 46, 47
law courts 24, 26, 27

M

Macedonia 42, 45
Marathon, Battle of 8, 14
mathematics 29, 45
medicine 10, 42
merchants 10, 24, 25
Minoans 44
Mount Olympus 20
Mount Pentelicus 22
Myceneans 5, 44

N

navy 8, 9, 16
nobles 14, 16

O

Olympic Games 34, 43
ostracism 17, 47

P

Panathenaia (festival) 36-7, 47
Parthenon 18, 19, 22, 25, 37, 43, 45, 47
Peloponnesian War 45
Pericles 45
Persia, Persians 6, 8, 12, 14, 18, 44, 45
philosophy, philosophers 5, 29, 45, 47
Phormion, Battle of 14
Piraeus 9, 13
pottery 17, 27, 31, 35, 38
public speaking 17, 42

R

Romans 42, 45
Roman Empire 42

S

sacrifice 20, 21, 37, 40, 47
Salamis, Battle of 9, 14
sanctuaries 18, 19
science, scientists 5, 29, 42, 45
slaves 16, 22, 25, 28, 29, 30-1, 32, 38, 47
soldiers 8, 12, 13, 14, 15, 40, 46, 47
Sparta 14, 45
sports 5, 29, 34-5, 37, 43, 47
statues 5, 18, 19, 37, 40

T

temples 9, 18, 19, 20, 21, 22-3, 24, 25, 32, 37, 39, 45, 46
theaters 32-3, 42
Thebes 45
Themosticles (General) 8, 13, 17
trade 6, 24, 25, 30
trials 26, 27
Troy, Trojans 6, 44
Trojan Horse 6
Trojan War 44

U

Underworld 40, 47

W

writers, poets 6, 13, 33, 44
war 5, 6, 14-15, 17, 20, 25, 34, 40
warships 5, 8, 9, 14, 15, 45, 47
weapons 5, 12, 14, 20, 38, 39, 44
women 16, 24, 25, 28, 30, 31, 32, 38, 40
workshops 9, 30, 38-9